PORSCHE

Randy Leffingwell

Motorbooks International
Publishers & Wholesalers

Dedication:
For my friend Dale von Trebra

First published in 1995 by Motorbooks International Publishers & Wholesalers, PO Box 2, 729 Prospect Avenue, Osceola, WI 54020 USA

Motorbooks International books are also available at discounts in bulk quantity for industrial or sales-promotional use. For details write to Special Sales Manager at the Publisher's address

Library of Congress Cataloging-in-Publication Data
Leffingwell, Randy
    Porsche / Randy Leffingwell.
      p.   cm. — (Enthusiast color series)
    Includes index.
    ISBN 0-87938-992-3
    1. Porsche automobile—History. I. Title. II.Series.
TL215.P75L442 1995
629.222'2—dc20   94-44211

On the front cover: The 1967 Typ 911R was one of Porsche's best kept secrets; production was limited to only twenty copies after the four prototypes proved their worth. Ferdinand Piëch intended the cars to be rolling test beds for new ideas and engine/drivetrain combinations.

On the frontispiece: Engine detail from the 1965 Typ 904/8 Bergspyder.

On the title page: Porsche's rally efforts produced memorable cars, like this 1970 Typ 911ST. Porsches wheeled to victory in the 1968, 1969, and 1970 Monte Carlo rallies.

On the back cover: The 1988 Typ 959 U.S. Sport featured a six-speed transmission that allowed the car to reach nearly 200mph. Only 229 were built including prototypes.

Printed and bound in Hong Kong

Contents

ACKNOWLEDGMENTS

My thanks for help in the production of this book go to Dick Barbour, San Diego, California; Jurgen Barth, Dr.Ing.h.c.F. Porsche AG., Weissach, Germany; Bob Cagle, San Diego, California; Bob Carlson, Porsche Cars North America, Reno, Nevada; Otis Chandler, Ojai, California; Tom Chang, Granada Hills, California; Warren Eads, Novato, California; Ernst Freiberger, EFA-Automobil Museum, Amerang, Germany; Fred Hampton, London, England; Ray Fulcher, San Juan Capistrano, California; Michael Hagen, Anaheim, California; Matt Harrington, Los Angeles, California; Dr. Warren Helgesen, Pasadena, California; Dr. William Jackson, Denver, Colorado; Dirk Layer, Vail, Colorado; Gerry Layer, San Diego, California; Michael Lederman, Parma, Italy; Robert Linton, New York City, New York; Jakob Maier, Amerang, Germany; Marco Marinello, Zurich, Switzerland; Kent Morgan, Arcadia, California; Dave Morse, Campbell, California; Kerry Morse, Tustin, California; John and Ray Paterek, Chatham, New Jersey; Helmut Pfeifhofer, Porsche Auto-Museum, Gmünd, Austria; Vasek Polak, Hermosa Beach, California; Jerry Reilly, Hardwick, Massachusetts; Peter Schneider, Dr.Ing.h.c.F.Porsche GmbH, Stuttgart-Zuffenhausen, Germany; Jerry Sewell, Newbury Park, California; Dick Simmons, Lake San Marcos, California; Paul Ernst Strähle, Schorndorf, Germany; Carl Thompson, Hermosa Beach, California; Bruce Trenery, Emeryville, California; and Derrick Walker, Warrington, Pennsylvania.

1948 Gmünd coupe **Holzmodel, opposite page**
Formed of ash, a holzmodel, *or wood form model, of the Gmünd coupe sits outside the Porsche Auto-Museum in Gmünd, Austria. The original form was broken up and burned for winter heating long ago. Museum owner Helmut Pfeifhofer used original drawings to pattern his replica.*

Chapter One

Early Days: Perfecting the Four-Cylinder

On December 1, 1930, Dr. Ferdinand Porsche placed a bet on the rest of his life when he opened his own engineering and design firm. The Austrian-born engineer was fifty-five years old. He had spent thirty-five years employed by other companies, producing electric and gasoline engines and trucks and cars. His accomplishments and reputation were good enough that he felt confident of his future. He had come to consider industrial Stuttgart, Germany, as his home even though he was born in agricultural Zell am See, Austria. While he earned his engineering doctorate from Vienna Technical Institute, he had received an honorary doctorate from the Technical University in Stuttgart. Now, after several years with Austro-Daimler and Steyr, car makers in Vienna, he returned to Stuttgart to start his own company. His twenty-one-year-old son Ferry joined in the effort.

To keep the work organized, Porsche numbered each job he undertook. Suspecting that no client would feel comfortable being a design/engineer's first project, he began his first commission, (a 2.0-liter car for the Wanderer company) and arbitrarily numbered it Typ 7. Work continued to come in. A Grand Prix race car for Auto Union was Typ 22. Later a 29ft long, six-wheeled Daimler-Benz land speed record attempt car was Typ 80.

Porsche's interest in affordable cars for the masses matched an ambition of Germany's leader, Adolph Hitler, for whom Porsche's design firm had already done other work. At the 1934 Berlin auto show, Hitler announced plans to introduce a "people's car", a *Volkswagen*. Porsche's firm was to produce three prototypes.

Prosperity led Porsche to move to suburban Zuffenhausen in June 1938. His staff numbered 176 workers designing, testing, and assembling automobiles. In 1940, Dr. Porsche

1955 Typ 550/1500RS Spyder, opposite page
Designed by Erwin Komenda, ninety of these aluminum-bodied racers were produced by Wendler Karosserie, and first examples appeared in August 1953. Ernst Fuhrmann's Carrera four-cam engine produced 110hp at 6200rpm, and was capable of propelling these 1,298lb two-seaters to 125mph.

1948 Gmünd coupe Holzmodel, next page
The coupes were fabricated out of aluminum by a panel beater named Freidrich Weber working for Professor Ferdinand Porsche. The aluminum panels were bent and hammered into the contours of the wood form and then welded together.

1952 America Roadster
Stripped to bare metal for panel restoration prior to painting and reassembly, these aluminum panels gleam under bright lights. Porsche produced three series of America Roadsters, at the instigation of Viennese-transplant Johnny Von Neumann who had resettled in southern California. Von Neumann wanted a lightweight car to race and wanted a roadster body style because of climate. The bodies were fabricated by Heinrich Gläser Karosserie in Wieden-Ullersicht near Nuremberg. Gläser built sixteen such bodies.

received the honorary title of Professor, again from Stuttgart's Technical University.

Porsche created the Volkswagen in Zuffenhausen. Other government projects, including tanks and armored weapons, were born there as well. But the German military command could not protect the firm during Allied bombing raids. When the factory was damaged in April 1944, Porsche set out to save his company. While the headquarters stayed in Stuttgart, engineering, design, and assembly works went to Austria. Modest production began in a sawmill in Gmünd, 100 miles south of Vienna. When the war ended, Ferry Porsche moved to Gmünd.

Work done for the German government before the War came back to haunt Professor Porsche and his family. Porsche was first and foremost an engineering firm intent on staying in business; the government was one of few paying clients. The Professor, notoriously apolitical, refused to salute Germany's commander-in-chief and, to Hitler's continued annoyance, always referred to him only as Herr Hitler. Still all the men in the Porsche family, including his daughter Louise's husband Dr. Anton Piëch, were arrested by the French in mid-1945 and questioned about their activities. Ferry was released almost immediately but it was another two years before it became

1955 356A GS-Carrera

The Carrera's engine was introduced in the 550 Spyder racing cars and its name came from the Mexican road races that Porsche won in 1953 and 1954. But according to Engineer Ernst Fuhrmann, his Typ 547 twin-cam flat-four engine, his first design project, was meant not only to race but also to fit into his own high-speed road car.

1955 356A GS-Carrera
The Typ 356 body design was penned by Porsche's designer and friend Erwin Komenda. Its round compound curves set the style for every Porsche since. Referred to as an "organic shape," it has very few straight lines.

1956 Typ 356A "LeMans Coupe" replica, right
Oregonian Gary Emory created the "European" replica for his own amusement, even fitting a 2-liter 914 engine that was modified to resemble the Fuhrmann flat four. Porsche wore No. 45 at LeMans in 1953 on a Typ 550 coupe with louvered panels instead of rear windows.

1956 Typ 356A "LeMans Coupe" replica, opposite page
Born of a cannibalized 356A coupe, enough parts were missing from this car that its restorer enjoyed artistic license and recreated a Gmünd-style LeMans bodywork. Louvered side panels replaced the rear windows and were welded in place. Plexiglas duct work feeds air into the engine.

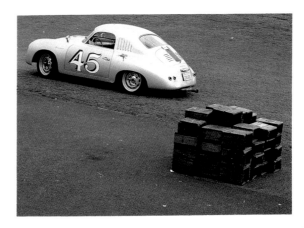

clear that the Porsches were engineers, not warriors, and they were released. Prior to that, Louise Piëch—who was running the 200-employee operations at Gmünd along with her brother Ferry—accepted a commission from Italian car maker Piero Dusio to design a Formula One Grand Prix racer for his Cisitalia firm. Porsche's concept used a water-cooled V-12 engine positioned behind the driver. The engine used dual overhead camshafts, a supercharger, and a five-speed transmission that could operate with four-wheel drive. The firm used Dusio's first payment to free Prof. Porsche and Dr. Piëch.

After two years in a cold prison in solitary confinement, Prof. Porsche, nearly seventy-two, was quite ill. When he returned to Gmünd, his primary goal was to produce a sports car bearing his name. At the Swiss Grand Prix in July 1948, the European press saw the first Porsche, a mid-engined, tubular space-frame car using mostly Volkswagen components. Hand assembled in Gmünd, the aluminum-bodied two-seat roadster, Typ 356-001, reached 85mph with a modified 1.1-liter VW engine.

Purely open cars were impractical for Europe. Through Dr. Anton Piëch, a Swiss hotel owner offered Porsche financial backing, and this allowed new design work and assembly to begin. The coupes that resulted, while still aluminum bodied, differed in configuration from the first roadster. The coupe's engine was placed behind the rear wheels to accommodate occasional passengers (or more luggage) behind the front seats. Ferry Porsche set a goal of producing 500 cars but its start was inauspicious; only four coupes

were assembled in 1948. About sixty of these Gmünd coupes were completed by 1952.

Journalists loved the car. Its high price insured the coupe an exclusive audience appeal. Response at the 1950 auto shows hinted that sales would come. Porsche moved back to Stuttgart and arranged with Reutter Karosserie to build steel car bodies. When Prof. Porsche turned seventy-five in September 1950, more than 250 cars had been sold. When he died of a stroke in 1951, his car and his company were on their way. Three years later 5,000 Porsche Typ 356s had been sold.

In 1952 Porsches were offered with three engines, the wildest being a 1.5-liter overhead-valve version designed by a recently hired, young Viennese engineer, Ernst Fuhrmann. This engine could push the rounded coupes to 100mph. A year later fully-synchronized transmissions and larger diameter brakes were offered as well. A convertible followed.

Porsche encouraged racing. It recognized that stories in newspapers about the accomplishments of drivers like Austrian Otto Mathé and others created interest that Porsche could not afford in advertising. Enthusiasm spread throughout the world and took hold strongly in the United States.

1958 1600 Speedster hardtop, opposite page
California distributor Johnny Von Neumann "invented" the Speedster as a car he could sell at a price to compete with Jaguar's XK120. Von Neumann pressed the U.S. importer Max Hoffman to convince the factory to build the car. To meet the $3,000 price, there was little standard equipment but many extra cost options including a hard top.

1958 1600 Speedster hardtop, above
Von Neumann conceived of the speedster as a "boulevard race car," so the boys could cruise Sunset or Hollywood Boulevards and the girls could see them. Options included a heater, sun visors, a tachometer, padded seats, carpeting, and a variety of engines.

1958 1600 Speedster hardtop, left
Reutter Karosserie cleaned up the lines of the standard 356 cabriolets and built the bodies right alongside the Porsche works in Zuffenhausen. With the removable hardtop and windshield detached, the Speedsters reminded first time viewers of an inverted bathtub.

1958 1600 Speedster hardtop, above
*The Speedsters were powered by 60hp 1600
Normal or 75hp Super engines. The 1600 Normal
with hardtop sold new for about $4,250. Ernst
Fuhrmann's 100hp Carrera engine also was available
at a premium price. Carrera-GS Speedsters sold
new for $5,260.*

1958 Typ 718RSK Formula 2, right
*The first RSK appeared at the Nurburgring in May
1957, but the versions with optional center-steering
position for hill-climbs or FIA Formula 2 races did not
exist until 1958. There were only two factory team
cars, and the other four were sold to privateers for
$8,000.*

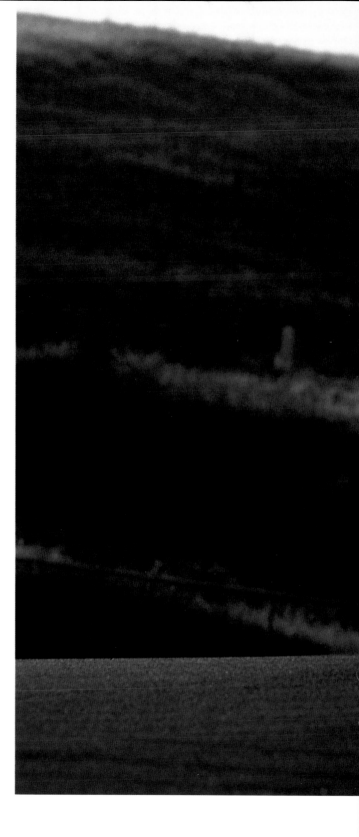

1958 Typ 718RSK Formula 2
The sleek Wendler aluminum bodies covered Ernst Fuhrmann's 1,498cc Typ 547/3 Carrera engine. Breathing through two Weber carburetors, the engine produced 148hp at 7500rpm. Weighing only 1,166lb, the cars easily reached 150mph. Conversion from left-side to center-steering took four hours.

Distributor Max Hoffman had brought Mercedes-Benz, Jaguar and other makes to the U.S. He saw Porsche as a new prospect for his customers. Hoffman's West Coast distributor Johnny Von Neumann was a racer first and salesman second. At Von Neumann's urging and Hoffman's pressure, Zuffenhausen produced a small run of sixteen aluminum-bodied America Roadsters in 1952. These were truly Porsche's first purpose-built racing cars. Victories by drivers like Jack McAfee, Ken Miles, and others, reported in American newspapers, did as much for Porsche in the U.S. as racing had done in Europe. Within another three years, as interest grew, Von Neumann visited Hoffman again.

Von Neumann wanted another open car—closed cars were too hot for California—but he wanted one for the streets to sell for $3,000. Von Neumann and Hoffman felt it was necessary to fight the price and performance competition offered by Triumph, Austin-Healey, and Jaguar. After Reutter slightly redesigned the roadster body and stripped every accessory from it, Porsche delivered its new low-slung Speedster for $2,995. They sold like mad. Owners paid extra for everything: tachometers, padded seats, floor mats, sun visors, cigarette lighters, heaters, and even clip-on hardtops. Produced from 1955 through 1959, Porsche sold more than 3,600 Speedsters. A docile 1500cc Normal 60hp engine was available. So was Ernst Fuhrmann's new four-cam Carrera-engined GS-GT package with 100hp. Not only did the name "Speedster" enter enthusiast jargon, but so did the car's shape, which resembled an overturned bathtub.

1960 356B 1600GTL Abarth Carrera
Only twenty-one of the Zagato designed, Abarth-built aluminum-bodied FIA Gran Turismo category competitors were assembled. Its looks defy its scale. It appears much longer than its 157in and much lower than its 52in height. German racer Paul Ernst Strähle made racing history many times in three different Abarth Carreras.

1960 356B 1600GTL Abarth Carrera
The Abarth's were fitted with the Typ 692/3A engines, with bore and stroke of 87.5x66mm for total displacement of 1,587cc. Carburetion was either Solex or Weber, and dual distributors were driven off the crankshaft. The twin-cam engines produced 135hp at 7300rpm.

The Fuhrmann Carrera engine (Typ 547) was introduced in 1953 for use in the Typ 550-1500RS racers, the Spyders. Throughout Europe and America, Spyders became the car to race if the racer wanted to win. In some events they made up almost the entire field. Spyders evolved into Typ 718s, the RSKs. The "K" came from the shape of a front suspension modification that proved unsuccessful. But the name persisted even though subsequent RS-60s and RS-61s reverted to a safer suspension configuration. Design improvements such as dual distributors and enormous Weber carburetors coaxed more than 150hp out of the flat-four Carrera. The 718s earned countless wins. Fitted with an optional center-steering position, these cars tantalized Porsche with the possibilities in international Formula Two and Formula One racing. In 1961, the beautiful Typ 804 introduced an extremely complicated flat-eight cylinder 1.5-liter engine designed by Hans Mezger. Sadly, it came up short of its competitors. Superb driving by teammates Dan Gurney and Jo Bonnier saved Porsche from humiliation, but the costs far exceeded the benefits, and Porsche withdrew from Formula One at the end of 1961. Other projects needed the resources.

As the fifties progressed, more luxury was offered for the road cars. Fitted luggage was optional, and a bench seat could be ordered, particularly on the 1955 U.S.-only model called the Continental. Lincoln protested the name, citing plans to reintroduce its own Continental in 1956. Initial U.S. exclusivity of the Speedster and Continental models miffed German buyers, and a "European" coupe model arrived in 1956.

1962 Typ 804 Formula 1

Successes in Formula 2 between 1958 and 1961 gave Porsche the courage to contest Formula 1 with this clean-lined single-purpose machine. Unfortunately, the effort was premature, the complex engine not yet powerful enough for competition. Its greatest victory was before a hometown crowd here at the Solitude Race Circuit in Stuttgart.

1962 Typ 804 Formula 1
The tiny cigar barely fit American racer Dan Gurney who recalled sticking out of it like a giraffe. It sat not quite 32in tall, barely 12ft long, and weighed only 1,010lb. Three were built, the second team car driven by Swede Jo Bonnier with a third car as team back up.

The 356A introduced in 1956 brought more modifications and improvements to the coupes and cabriolets. These all-steel bodies were fitted with a curved windshield. A gas gauge was standard equipment. Porsche reduced wheel size from 16in to 15in. In 1958, it offered a new convertible built by Drauz Karosserie in Heilbronn near Stuttgart. This Convertible D provided roll-up windows and a taller top than the Reutter Speedsters.

In late 1959, Porsche first showed the Model 356B, the T-5 body, that could be ordered with the new Super 90 engine. Then in 1961 the T-6 body was introduced; the windshield and rear window were larger, the front deck lid squared off to increase luggage capacity, and the fuel filler cap was removed to the fender. Owners could now refill the tank without opening the trunk. The Carrera 2 was introduced in September 1961. This 2-liter four-cam engine produced 130hp and had evolved from Ernst Fuhrmann's 1.5-liter Typ 547 as Porsche's most powerful street engine yet.

July 1963 brought the 356C with race-proven four-wheel disc brakes. Three engines were available, the 1600C, 1600SC, and the Carrera 2. A total of 450 of the Carrera 2s were sold, overlapping from 356Bs to Cs. Then two months later in September, the Typ 901 was shown at the Frankfurt Auto Show. This car introduced a new shape and the opposed-six-cylinder engine. The 356C and SC remained on sale through late 1965. Production of the Typ 901 began in late 1964, renumbered Typ 911 after Peugeot claimed its right to production car designations with "0" in the middle.

The Typ 901 was conceived in the late 1950s. Each iteration of the flat-four cylinder engine was thought to be its last and best. The 356's ten-year-old round shape contrasted with longer, swoopy Jaguars, Ferraris, and Corvettes. Still, sales of the organic-shaped cars held steady and Porsche hesitated to fix something that seemed unbroken.

1962 Typ 804 Formula 1
The magnificently complex Typ 753 flat eight-cylinder needed 195 to 200hp but, hard as engineer Hans Mezger worked, it never exceeded 180hp at 9200rpm. Formula 1 in those days had a 1.5-liter displacement limitation. The Typ 753 had a 66x54.6mm bore and stroke for a total of 1,494cc.

1964 356SC Cabriolet, previous page right
Beginning in 1963 with the introduction of the 356C models, four-wheel disc brakes, manufactured by ATE, were standard equipment, requiring different wheels. Otherwise the C-model cars were virtually identical to late production 356Bs (known as the T-6 bodies). Twin air-grilles were most noticeable. The 356B and C models brought the fuel tank filler outside to the passenger's front fender and enlarged the front trunk lid to improve access.

1964 356SC Cabriolet, above
Underneath the car, a slightly thicker anti-roll bar, along with slightly softer rear torsion bars, improved handling. Adjustable Koni shock absorbers were standard on SC models. The 356SC used Porsche's Typ 616/16 engine with twin Solex carburetors to produce 95hp at 5800rpm. The standard 1600C engine produced 75hp at 5200rpm.

1964 356SC Cabriolet

Recaro seats were a key element in Porsche comfort. In March 1964, Porsche acquired Reutter Carosserie, its neighboring coach builder. Seat production was retained by the newly formed Recaro group, a name formed from the first letters of each word. The 356SC interior comfort was further aided by improving heating, defrosting, and ventilation. The cabriolets were popular and over the final three years of production, from 1963 through 1964, more than 3,100 were produced.

Chapter Two

BIGGER ENGINES, GREATER SUCCESSES

Ferdinand Alexander Porsche ("Butzi"), Ferry's twenty-eight-year old son, joined the firm in May 1957 and worked through his father's design education process. Butzi became head of a styling department of seven people in 1958. His education culminated in his forming the shapes of the 901 street car and Typ 904 Carrera GTS racing car. Using plasticine, a car modeler's clay-like material, he created the 904 on a tight deadline that allowed no changes. The production car was done on a more relaxed schedule.

Money no longer devoted to Formula One racing permitted further engineering developments in the 901 that improved steering geometry and suspension. Excluding some minor enhancements (engine air-intake vents were moved from the fenders to the rear deck lid), Butzi's original ideas hit showrooms nearly intact. Two models were offered. A four-cylin-

1964 Typ 904 Carrera GTS, opposite page
Many racers and designers regard the Carrera GTS as the most aesthetically pure race car design ever. Wearing No. 86, this car, 904-006, won the Targa Florio in April 1964, was twelfth at Nurburgring in May, and third in GT class at LeMans in June. In January 1965, it took second overall in the Monte Carlo Rally and launched Porsche's rally career.

der version using a detuned 356SC engine was called the 912 and was introduced in the U.S. for $4,690 while the 911 sold for $6,490. Half of the first year production was destined for the U.S. market.

Porsche's last four-cylinder 356SC cabriolets were sold in 1965. The need for a new open car model was apparent. Californian Johnny Von Neumann commissioned Italian designer Nuccio Bertone to produce a prototype. The new 911 chassis proved to be not stiff enough for a completely open car. Butzi Porsche's solution, announced in September 1965, was heralded as "The world's first safety convertible." Rather than disguise its integral roll-over bar, the Targa model—named to honor the Sicilian road race—emphasized it in brushed stainless steel. A roll-up canvas top and separate plastic window could be removed and stored in the trunk. By 1968, a hard rear window was available, the Sportomatic semi-automatic transmission was introduced, and several new interior and engine packages were offered. The 911T (touring), 911L (luxury) and 911S (sport) were introduced. (U.S. exhaust emission standards required modifications that delayed the 911S arrival until 1969.)

1964 Typ 904 Carrera GTS
It began as a question: could Porsche make an entire car in plastic? FIA's Group 3 offered possibilities, and in November 1962, parameters were set for the Typ 904. Working in Plasticine, a car modeler's clay, Butzi Porsche shaped the lines. Four months later the first prototype was driven.

The 911L and 912 were discontinued in 1969, the latter to prepare for the arrival of the 914 mid-engine car. A fuel-injected Model 911E (Einspritzung—injection—in German) filled the middle range. It provided less luxury than the now-fuel-injected S model but gave comparable performance. A major handling improvement resulted from lengthening the wheelbase by 47mm—nearly two inches—behind the front seats.

From 1965 through 1969, Porsche racing achieved ever greater accomplishments. In 1965 Louise Piëch's son, twenty-nine-year old Ferdinand, was named head of engineering and development. For Piëch, outright overall victory was the only objective. Class

1964 Typ 904 Carrera GTS

The no-frills interior left the fiberglass showing. On early cars, the roll bar was not incorporated into the fiberglass body and fit outside the back window glass in notches in the rear bodywork. The entire car weighed 1,433lb; it was capable of 0–60mph in 5.5sec and, depending on gearing, more than 155mph at the top end.

1964 Typ 904 Carrera GTS

Development chief Hans Tomala planned the car to use the new Typ 901 210hp flat six-cylinder engine. But familiarity with the flat fours and the worldwide prevalence of spare parts suggested otherwise. So 116 production models were built using the Typ 587/3A 2.0-liter, 180hp engines—plus a few four- and six-cylinder prototypes—before a final run of cars used the six-cylinder race engine, all mounted ahead of the rear axle.

1965 Typ 904/8 Bergspyder
What it lacked in grace and style, it made up for in punch. This is the first of five Bergspyders—or open mountain-racers—that engineer Ferdinand Piëch ordered as the new head of engineering and development. Barely 130in long but with 240hp on hand, the car jumped— hence its nickname the Kanguruh.

victories—in the 2.0-liter-and-under categories—were no longer enough. As such, a progression of exciting racing cars appeared. And these brought results.

Butzi Porsche's lovely Carrera GTS was conceived and designed to accommodate racing versions of the Typ 901 six-cylinder production engine. Development problems delayed this through 1964 but in 1965, the first 904/6 coupes appeared, supplemented by Piëch's ugly, stubby, aggressive 904/8 Bergspyders ("mountain spyders," primarily for hill climb racing). These tiny 11ft. long, 1,154lb cars used Porsche's Typ 771 2-liter flat-8 cylinder 240hp engine. The first car was nicknamed *Kanguruh* because of its handling. In 1966, the striking Carrera 6s (Typ 906) appeared, quickly nicknamed the *Batmobile* by photographers who appreciated its gull-wing type doors. Sleek 906s raced at LeMans with aerodynamic tails more than two feet longer than normal *Batmobiles.*

Piëch remained interested in hill climbs. The 904 chassis needed improvement and so a tubular space frame and slightly longer wheelbase evolved into the Typ 910 in 1966. For hill climbs, the 910s continued to use the Typ 771 engines first seen in the 904/8; versions of the Typ 901 flat six were used for endurance races. With Hans Herrmann and Jo Siffert driving, a 6-cylinder 910 finished 4th overall at the Daytona 24-hours, and Gerhardt Mitter and Scooter Patrick finished third at Sebring behind two 7-liter Ford GTs. Typ 906s were sold to privateers from the beginning, but Porsche decided against selling 910s. As factory entries in prototype classes,

1965 Typ 904/8 Bergspyder
Porsche's flat eight-cylinder Typ 711 displaced 1,991cc from 76x54.6mm bore and stroke. Four Weber 48 IDF carburetors and 10.4:1 compression produced 240bhp at 8500rpm. From a standstill, the Kanguruh *reached 100km/h in 4.8sec. Driver's with sufficient courage topped 150mph.*

the 910s did not compete directly against customers in 906s who would have chafed at the cost of needing a new car to remain competitive each year.

In 1967, Piëch, intrigued by the 911, created four prototypes and twenty production versions of a lightweight racing Typ 911R. These innocuous white coupes used lighter body and window panels. They became development test beds for engine and transmission variations. Between 1967 and 1970 911Rs won countless races, rallies, and world endurance records running with carbureted or fuel-injected 906 engines and even Sportomatic semi-automatic transmissions.

Eight-cylinder racing engines reappeared in 1967 in the Typ 907s. These also achieved

1965 Typ 904/8 Bergspyder
Introduced in time for the 1965 Targa Florio, the 904 GTS sheet-steel-based chassis supported an all fiberglass body. Without driver but with fuel, the car weighed 1,254lb. Gerhard Mitter and Colin Davis bounced and fought it to 2nd overall in the seven-hour Sicilian road race.

numerous overall victories. Hans Mezger developed their 2.2-liter versions from his complex Grand Prix engine, replacing Weber carburetors with Bosch mechanical fuel injection. The 907's slightly smaller bodies evolved from lessons in aerodynamics learned from the 904, 906, and 910. The Typ 908s appeared in 1968. Powered by Mezger's 3.0-liter flat eights, the 908s continued Piëch's assault on overall victories. Porsche produced 908 long-tail coupes for endurance races such as Daytona and LeMans and followed with two short-tail versions, the 908/2—known as *Flounder* for its undulating body—and the 908/3, which introduced wind-tunnel aerodynamics to Porsche racing. The stubby 908/3 soon showed its cleanly cut, truncated tail to the racing world.

The 908/3s ran away with events such as the Targa Florio, the 1000km of Nurburgring, and many others. Yet the factory 908L lost the 1968 LeMans (third behind Swiss racers Rico Steinemann and Dieter Spoerry in their own 907) by 100 meters after 24-hours to a five-liter Ford GT. A Federation International Automobile (FIA) Group 5 and 6 rule change for 1969 was meant only to extend the life of existing cars such as Ford's GT40 and Ferrari's 250LMs, 330s, and 512s. However, Piëch found a loophole. Through it, he served notice on the rest of the racing world. **39**

1967 Typ 911R

Engineering chief Ferdinand Piëch used the 911R to answer questions: how light can we make it, how hard can we push it, how long will it last? Its highest achievement: 12,505 miles in ninety-six hours at more than 125mph, plus sixteen other records during the same run. In 1968, a specially constructed car won the Marathon de la Route using the Sportomatic transmission. And in 1969, another car using a special fuel-injected prototype engine won both the Tour de France and the Tour de Corse.

1967 Typ 911R, right

Standard fare for the "production" 911R was the Typ 901/22 2-liter flat six, with bore and stroke of 80x66mm. Using two Weber 46IDA3C carburetors, 210hp at 8000rpm was claimed. Free-flow resonators gave the 911R a distinctive exhaust note.

1972 Typ 911S Targa
When the last 356C cabriolets were produced in 1965, Porsche was left without an open car. California distributor Johnny Von Neumann proposed a prototype Bertone-designed spyder, but he knew the 911 chassis was not stiff enough. While Bertone fabricated, Ferdinand Alexander "Butzi" Porsche, designer of the 911, solved the problem with a built-in roll bar.

Hans Mezger reviewed drawings for the Cisitalia 12-cylinder engine from Gmünd. From this he designed Porsche's Typ 912, its most formidable engine ever. This was the 4.5-liter, air-cooled, fuel-injected flat 12-cylinder for the Typ 917 racing cars. The new rules for Group 5 and 6 required a "production" of twenty-five cars or more with a maximum engine size of 5-liters. Ferrari and Ford each had plenty of 512s and GT40s. Racing fans loved the battle between Modena and Dearborn, and track owners loved full grandstands. The FIA hoped to keep everyone happy while saving manufacturers the cost of developing new cars. The FIA never expected Porsche's 917s.

1972 Typ 911S Targa

Porsche's racing and high-performance models have frequently been named in honor of the company's first international victory in Mexico at the Carrera PanAmericana. When time came to name Porsche's steel-banded, stiffer cabriolet, Press Chief Evi Butz suggested honoring company wins in Sicily at the Targa Florio.

The twenty-five 917s—assembled only enough to pass FIA inspection—came together hastily. There was no track or wind tunnel testing. After the cars were homologated they were dismantled to undergo further development, as was usual with any racing car. A few prototypes were taken out for track testing. Their long tails revealed a diabolical nature. The design team directed by Helmut Flegl had taken each previous successful design, the 906, 907, and 908, and moved on. But the longtail designs had succeeded by luck. Under hard acceleration the 917's nose tended to lift. Worse, under braking, its elongated teardrop shape provided too little downforce, and the rear end lifted, whipping the back of the car. Seasoned racers quickly nicknamed the 917s. Brian Redman called it the *Widow-maker*, Gerhard Mitter named it the *Ulcer*, and Vic Elford referred to it as a "monster."

A mid-season test session at Zeltweg, Austria, revealed the solutions. The Canadian-American Challenge (Can-Am) racing series in North America gave birth to 917 Spyders with lines based on the 908/3. At Zeltweg, a Spyder using the coupes' chassis, engine, and drivers, lapped the track four seconds quicker than the coupes. It had none of the coupe's evil handling. Gulf Oil provided sponsorship for the 1970 European season and team Manager John Wyer, John Horseman and others joined Flegl in creating a solution at Zeltweg. The teardrop end of the first coupes was filled out to match the fuller, stubby end of the Spyder; the 917K (for Kurz, German for short) was born at Zeltweg and the problems were largely solved. Engine and gearbox reliability was improved as well and the 917s began winning races before the end of 1969. Ferdinand Piëch's goal of the Manufacturer's World Championship seemed within reach for 1970.

But the costs of developing and racing the 908s and 917s had grown unsupportable. A financial meeting revealed that 30 million DM had been spent on all forms of racing in 1969. In a shrinking economy, this was no longer possible for a family-held business. Piëch's dream could only come true through complete sponsorship from outside sources such as Gulf Oil. Factory racing development was stopped. Piëch's reason-for-being was taken away. A split occurred between the Porsches and Piëchs. Louise Piëch returned to Salzburg to concentrate on her Austrian distributorship; from there Ferdinand could continue to campaign 908s and 917s as a privateer through Porsche Salzburg. With Martini & Rossi sponsorship, he raced against the factory team in Gulf Oil colors.

1972 Typ 911S Targa
U.S.-specification 911S 2.4-liter engines used mechanical fuel injection. The 84x70.4mm Typ 911/53 flat-6 cylinder engine produced 190hp at 6500rpm, and the car weighed 2,365lb. In 1972 only, the dry sump oil filler was outside (below the Targa bar) on the passenger side. Too often, gas station attendants filled the sump with gasoline.

1972 Typ 911S Targa

Ironically, critics first called the stainless steel Targa band too flashy. Butzi Porsche responded that it was a structural element and no apology would be made for it. The customers should see improvements for which they reap benefits. The lightweight top removed easily and folded for storage.

Long-tail 917s were still run where higher top speed was more important than tight handling through corners. For LeMans 1970 and 1971, the Gulf team and the Martini-sponsored Salzburg team ran the 917Ls as well as shorter K-coupes. Piëch fulfilled his own dream for uncle Ferry Porsche's company: when 917 victories were tallied up, Porsche had won the World Championship of Makes both years.

In North America, Porsche won the Can-Am series with its Porsche+Audi-entered 917P+A Spyders. Engines grew from the 4.5-liter, 580hp coupe versions to 4.9-liters with twin turbochargers, producing 1000hp. In 1971 Mark Donohue and George Follmer, racing L&M-sponsored 917-10s for team owner Roger Penske, claimed the championship. For 1972, Donohue with Sunoco-sponsorship dominated the series in the Typ 917-30s. Using a 5.4-liter twin-turbocharged flat-12 with 1,300hp, the 240mph Porsche swept the series.

But the joys—and excesses—of the late 1960s and early 1970s caught up with motorsports. A worldwide recession, aided by the formation of the Organization of Petroleum Exporting Countries (OPEC), brought high-powered automobiles and racing into critical focus. Porsche sales in 1969 (15,000 cars

worldwide) shrunk one-third in 1970, to 10,000. U.S. distribution was reorganized with the introduction of Audi. Porsches previously were sold in facilities often owned by Volkswagen dealers. Now VW dealers had to build separate showrooms to sell Porsche and Audi. (It was to promote this relationship that the 1970 Can-Am entry was named the 917P+A).

"The cockpit was so narrow relative to the chassis—which was comparatively wide—we were sitting barely to the right of the centerline. The bit of the car that was reserved for the driver was pretty small!"

—Vic Elford on the 907K,
from Porsche Legends

1968 Typ 907K, opposite page
Ferdinand Piëch's new 907 moved the driver to the right side where the 906 and 910 still drove on the left. Much smaller than the 910, the 907 with its fighter-plane-type cockpit offered a 25 percent decrease in aerodynamic drag. Barely 159in long overall, it stood only 36.2in tall. The 907's Typ 771/1 flat-eight displaced 2,195cc with 80x54.6mm bore and stroke. Bosch mechanical fuel injectors helped produce 270hp at 8600rpm. With the Typ 907 five-speed transmission, the combination proved good for nearly 185mph in the 1,265lb two-seater.

1969 Typ 908LH, next page
One of three langheck (longtail) 908s, these 3-liter flat eight-cylinder powered prototypes produced 350hp and topped 200mph on the Mulsanne Straight at LeMans. The rear wings were controversial but required to tame a flight-prone rear end. The 908 came third to Ford's 5-liter GT40 in 1968—by a scant 100 meters after twenty-four hours.

1969 Typ 917K, previous page

Wearing 1970 Gulf Oil colors, the K benefited from aerodynamic improvements reached at the end of 1969 that eliminated a terrifying lift that occurred when drivers came off the gas pedal. The 917 was Porsche's answer to a new FIA ruling favoring existing cars, but the FIA never expected Porsche would produce a new car to take advantage of the rule change.

1969 Typ 917K, above

Hans Mezger's Typ 912/00 engine was the first version of his air-cooled flat 12-cylinder and produced 580hp at 8400rpm. The 4.5-liter, 85x66mm bore and stroke engine fitted dual overhead camshafts and used Bosch mechanical fuel injection. Eventually, the 5.4-liter Typ 917/12 provided another 80hp in a similar coupe body style.

1970 Typ 917L

English racer Vic Elford called the longtail a "monster" but loved it. He tamed the monster well enough to take it along Mulsanne flat out at 245mph at night in the rain without lifting from the gas through the "kink," a slight right bend. The 917s exemplified the coming of the end of an era in motorsports with no limits.

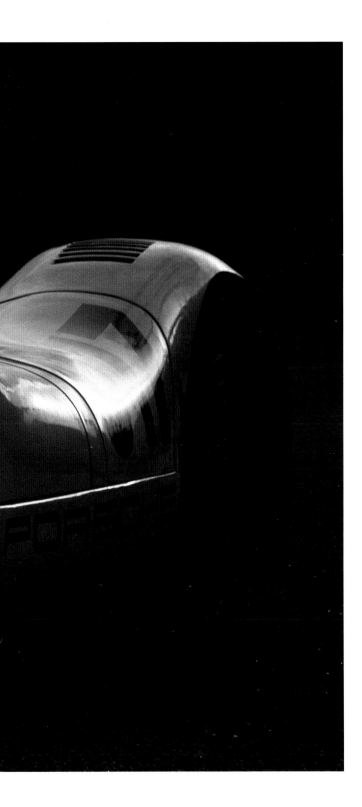

1970 Typ 917L
For Ferdinand Piëch, the 917 represented an all-out assault on the World Championship rather than merely another class victory. The undulating shapes were invented by design engineer Eugen Kolb and were graced, like fine art pieces, with Styling Chief Tony Lapine's memorable paint schemes.

"You couldn't change your mind if you'd committed it to a corner. If you'd made a mistake, you were pretty likely to have an accident."

—Vic Elford on the 917 long tail, from Porsche Legends

1972 Typ 917/30, *next page*
Mark Donohue made Can-Am history with the Sunoco 917/30, and Herbert Müller raced the InterSerie, a kind of European Can-Am series, with Martini-Rossi sponsorship. Running the Typ 912/51 engine—Hans Mezger's chef-d'oeuvre—Müller and Donohue had twin turbochargers and intercoolers at their disposal. With the boost up, nearly 1,300hp propelled the 1,760lb spyders .

Chapter Three

TAKING THE TURBO TO THE STREETS

In September 1969, Porsche introduced the Typ 914 at the Frankfurt Auto Show. Conceived in 1966 as a sports car project for Volkswagen, the mid-engine car came back to Porsche when VW management changed in late 1968. Porsche continued developing the car as a replacement for its 912. Derided in the European press as the Volks-Porsche, it used the VW411's 80hp 1.6-liter engine. A stronger version, the 914/6, used Porsche's 2-liter 110hp 911T engine. Over its lifetime, 3,353 of these 914/6 models sold. The 914/6 GT used Typ 901/35 engines. The oil cooler from the 908 was mounted in the nose, the suspension modified, and the chassis was stiffened. This work could be done at Zuffenhausen or pieces could be purchased from local dealers and installed by racers themselves. Factory entries won the 84-hour Marathon de la Route, and long-time Parisian

1973 Carrera RS, opposite page
A total of 1,580 Carrera RS 2.7 models were sold, 528 as Lightweight coupes in order to qualify it for racing. The engine, Typ 911/83, produced 210hp at 6300rpm and was bored out to 90x70.4mm. Front and rear bumpers, rear decklid, and burzel *ducktail spoiler were fiberglass, and the interior deleted all sound deadening material.*

distributor SonAuto won GT class at LeMans in 1970, averaging just 19mph less than the winning 917K. An extremely limited-production Typ 916 appeared in 1972. The cars used a 190hp 911S engine in a body with a welded-in-place steel roof and were only offered to Porsche family and friends. Just eleven of these mid-engine, leather-upholstered, $12,900 coupes were built in 1972.

In the boardroom another reorganization had occurred. Soon after the Piëchs and Porsches withdrew from actively running the company, Ernst Fuhrmann returned. The brilliant creator of the Carrera four-cam engine for the 356s had left Porsche in 1956 when further advancement seemed unlikely. After 15 years running another company Fuhrmann was hired to come back to Porsche as its Technical Director. He is an enthusiast who loves racing and high-performance engines. But he returned to a company where budget constraints severely limited what was possible, where a world economy doubted the need for expensive two-seat high performance cars, and where U.S. safety concerns became a consideration in future product design.

Porsche engines had grown from 2.2-liters to 2.4-liters. Plans existed to replace the

1970 914/6 GT, above
Porsche's long-time French distributor, SonAuto,
entered the 1970 LeMans with this factory-built
914/6 GT, driven to first in GT class, sixth overall,
by Guy Chasseuil and Claude Ballot-Lena. Averaging
99.3mph, they covered 2,382.5 miles on one set of
tires and brake pads.

1970 914/6 GT, right
Porsche created a virtual 906 racing engine for the
914/6 GT with the Typ 901/25. Its 80x66mm bore
and stroke displaced 1,991cc, and two Weber
46IDA3C carburetors helped achieve 220hp at
7800rpm. Cylinder heads featured larger valves,
a more aggressive camshaft, and twin-plugs with
transistorized ignition.

1970 914/6 GT, left

FIA regulations required that Gran Turismo entries carry a "passenger" seat with safety harness. Otherwise, the interior was a 914 stripped of all weight and nonessentials. The Typ 901 5-speed gearbox was fitted.

1970 914/6 GT, below

Front and rear deck lids and bumpers were plastic while the wide fender flares were steel welded directly to the structure. Wider wheels, 6x15s front and 7x15s rear, were responsible for grip and cornering during 1970 LeMans, which ran much of the night in the rain.

1970 Typ 911ST

The ST's in rally trim used the Typ 911/20 2.2 liter with 84x66mm bore and stroke. With Bosch mechanical fuel injection, the engines produced 180hp at 6500rpm. This 1970 ST was lightened before assembly using aluminum for the rear deck lid and doors and fiberglass for the front and rear bumpers and hood. It weighed barely 2,002lb. Three entries plus a spare were produced, this one winning Monte Carlo in 1970 with Bjorn Waldegaard driving and Lars Helmers as navigator.

911. But Fuhrmann knew that many Porsche buyers were repeat customers. These loyalists liked the car. He was not at Porsche when Piëch's 911Rs stretched the limits of the 911. But he knew the cars and had read the newspapers. It only remained for Fuhrmann to pump enthusiasm back into the product. Racing in Group 5 and 6 was out of the question, but competing in production-based Group 3 and 4 still earned newspaper coverage that brought buyers to the dealers.

So in October 1972, Porsche unveiled its 2.7-liter Carrera RS at the Paris auto show. It was jazzed up with script lettering along the sides and a new *burzel* (ducktail) on the rear deck lid to suggest its racing heritage. Sound deadening, undercoating, and interior insulation were deleted. Lightweight panels were used for front and rear deck lids. The engine, virtually new, produced 210hp (the 1972 production 911S used the 180hp 2.4-liter engine) and could push the RS to 155mph. Porsche had to build 500 to qualify for Group 4. All 500 sold at the Paris show. Another 500—with the insulation materials replaced that were deleted to qualify the 2,117lb lightweight racer—were built and sold immediately. Final sales counted 1,580 2.7 RS cars sold, a number that qualified it for Group 3 racing. Porsche's total worldwide sales returned to 15,000 cars that year.

For Group 4 the racing engineers produced a full-competition RSR version with 300hp. It won its very first race in February 1973, the Daytona 24-hours, only five months after the Paris show. But due to emissions and safety standards, the 2.7 RS was not legal in the U.S. It was not until 1974 that a 174hp **63**

1973 Carrera RS

Series production began in October 1972 for the Carrera RS 2.7-liter coupes, meant to return Porsche to racing without the costs of developing prohibitively expensive prototypes like the 917s again. The production versions, Group 4-legal, quickly led to RSR competition versions, raced days and nights through the next three years.

U.S. version was available to buyers. Not only was the engine modified, but 5-mph-impact bumpers and door side-impact reinforcements had to be installed as well.

The frontal impact of OPEC hit in 1974. Porsche reduced production to a three-day work week as output slipped below 9,000 cars including 914, 911S, and Carrera models.

Again, the life and future of the company—and the 911—were threatened. But Ernst Fuhrmann had started life as an engine designer, and he looked to the engines for the company's salvation. He saw that a legacy of wealthier times was the turbo that had brought success in the Can-Am and the Inter-Serie, Europe's version of the races. It seemed natural to him to incorporate this device that improved power output so greatly yet actually quieted the engine. The Typ 930, introduced in late 1974, shoe-horned a turbocharger into a jammed engine compartment and provided 260hp at 5500rpm. Europe got production cars in March 1975 while U.S. certification (emissions and safety again) delayed arrival until year's end. The *"burzel"* from the 2.7 RS was enlarged into a "whale tail" flat wing for both the 930 and the Carreras.

The U.S. market remained crucial. While emissions standards deprived the 911S and Carreras of 10hp (and an additional 5hp off for California-bound cars), the factory fitted other standard features and even priced the U.S.-bound cars lower than those destined for the German market. With the 930's U.S. arrival—renamed the 911 Turbo Carrera to replace the normally aspirated Carrera—U.S. sales exceeded half of all Porsches sold.

SACHS
Dick Barbour RACING
6
SACHS
CLUTCHES & GAS SHOCKS
GOODYEAR
GOODYEAR

Chapter Four

NEW ENGINES IN NEW LOCATIONS

From the early days, Porsche was the research and design arm for Volkswagen. A certain portion of VW's budget was allocated to Zuffenhausen and to Weissach (opened in 1971) for development of new models. When Fuhrmann returned to Porsche in 1971, the engineers had already begun work on a new VW project, EA425, a front-engine water-cooled fastback sport car. As with the Typ 914, events conspired to scuttle VW's ambitions. Political and economic considerations made the car too valuable to kill and EA425 reverted to Porsche to become its Typ 924. Production began in November 1975 using the 125hp fuel-injected VW engine. When the 924 was turbocharged for the 1979 model year, it boosted power to 170hp and the car performed nearer to expectations. (Ironically, at that time, emissions standards had so tightly hamstrung the turbo 930 that U.S. sales were discontinued.)

1980 Typ 935K3, opposite page
One of racing's most successful conglomerates merged Porsche of Weissach with Erwin Kremer of Cologne to produce a product managed and operated by Dick Barbour of California. In 1980, the Barbour Racing 935K3 took first in Group 5 at the Nurburgring 1000km and first in IMSA's GTX class at LeMans.

In late 1975, as the 924 and 930 became available to dealers, a racing version of the 930, the Typ 935, showed the motorsports world that Porsche was very much alive. Two factory-entered 935s, using a new turbocharged 2.86-liter flat-six with air-to-water intercooling, Bosch fuel-injection, and twin-plug ignition, were prepared for the 1976 racing season in Group 5. The 2,134lb cars had 590hp at 7900rpm to propel them to a few early—and encouraging—victories.

Racing engineer Norbert Singer was project manager for the 935, his first race car for Porsche. He was a master at reading and interpreting the FIA rules. For 1977 a change favored a competitor—until Singer understood that it did not prohibit him from making the same change and lowering the 935 by several inches. In 1977 Porsche began selling versions of its cars, the 935/77 (with 1976 specifications), to independent racers. Private teams such as Erwin Kremer in Cologne, Germany, and Bob Garretson and Dick Barbour in California bought cars and immediately modified them to try to beat the factory team in European and U.S-International Motor Sports Association (IMSA) events.

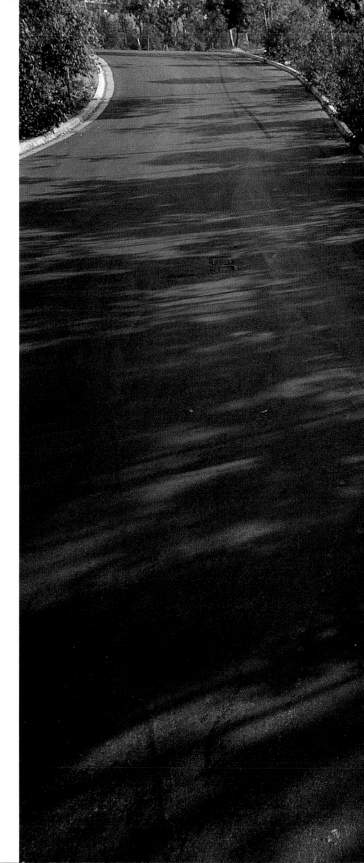

1980 Typ 935K3
Erwin Kremer performed more than 100 changes on the 935 including obvious bodywork modifications. Ekkehard Zimmermann of Design Plastic Company specified Kevlar for Kremer's new body pieces. He also added "fences" along the fenders to control airflow over the car.

For 1978 a new FIA rule allowed "aerodynamic appliances" which meant to Singer a whole new nose, tail, fenders, and doors and which meant to the world *Moby Dick*. FIA inspectors were stunned. Rules intended to ban such creations somehow had encouraged them. *Moby Dick* spawned a generation of aerodynamic appliances. Others copied the bodywork, and variations of *Moby Dick* quickly appeared. Then Kremer produced his legendary 935K3 and won eleven of twelve German National Championship races in 1979. Beginning in 1980, Kremer sold entire cars as well as kits to convert 935/77s into K3s. Dick Barbour bought a car and won IMSA's championship in 1980.

In mid-October 1975, while Weissach labored over the 935s, Ernst Fuhrmann asked Norbert Singer to consider the prototype regulations for Group 6. Fuhrmann suggested that old spare parts from the 917s could be "adapted". With eight months until LeMans and with French Renault and Italian Alfa-Romeo team prototypes already in preparation, Fuhrmann wanted again to be in the hunt—even while watching the budgets.

Some parts worked but much of the Typ 936 was completely new, produced almost overnight. When 1976 ended, the 520hp 3.0-liter, 1,540lb spyders won four outright

victories out of eight starts—including LeMans. This gave Porsche and Fuhrmann the championship for Group 6. The next year, the 936/77 won again at LeMans. And in 1981, in its final appearance, Fuhrmann's thoroughly updated five-year-old car developed from 917 parts, the 936/81, won again at LeMans.

The 924s raced as well. A 924 Carrera GT was introduced at the 1979 Frankfurt Auto Show. With a turbocharged, intercooled version of the 2.0-liter Audi-based in-line four-cylinder engine, the GT boasted 210hp. To qualify for Group 4, 400 were sold. Then fifty models of a higher-tuned Carrera GTS were produced and sold, followed by sixteen of the Typ 924 Carrera GTRs. In LeMans trim, these most-modified cars weighed 2,083lb, 800lb less than street 924 Turbos. With 375hp engines they reached nearly 180mph on Mulsanne. Porsche entered three GTRs in 1980, painted with the flags of its primary markets, Germany, the United States, and the United Kingdom. After twenty-four hours, much of it in rain, the 924s were still running. The best finish came from the German-flagged

1980 Typ 935K3
Plumbers nightmare—or brilliant design— Kremer used the flat fan and managed to fit an air-to-air-intercooler into cramped space as well. The endurance-tune 3-liter K3 engine produced 780hp at 8000rpm with twin KKK turbochargers. In LeMans dress, without fluids, the K3s weigh 2,270lb.

1980 Typ 935K3
Kremer stiffened the chassis through triangulated roll cage members to each shock absorber tower. The 935s started out with a production 911 steel chassis to which an aluminum tube roll cage was fitted, surrounded with fiberglass or Kevlar bodywork. Barbour race preparation was extremely tidy.

1981 B.F.Goodrich 924 Carrera GTR
At 4 p.m. Sunday, Porsche had again won LeMans, this time with its new 956. Minutes later, B.F. Goodrich's 924GTR #87 finished fifteenth after 2,307.9 miles at 96.2mph. The sister car, #86, retired in the eleventh hour. Racing in Group 5, Porsche produced only sixteen GTRs, after homologation was met with 400 924 Carrera GT models and fifty GTS versions.

car at sixth overall. The 924GTRs returned in 1981, entered by American tire maker B.F.Goodrich to promote a new high-performance street radial. Two factory 924s were entered as well; one of them was a 2,196lb 924 Carrera GTP that offered a hint of what production Porsche buyers could expect in the future. It was powered by a new 2.5-liter Porsche-designed, in-line four-cylinder engine with 410hp at 6500rpm. The GTP, precursor to the Typ 944 (and now generally referred to as the 944 GTP), finished seventh overall behind Fuhrmann's 936/81.

Both the 924GTP and the 936/81 ran new engines developed from other projects. The 936 used an engine spun off an ill-fated assault on the U.S. Indy car series, while the sixteen-valve 944 engine was one-half of a 5.0-liter V-8 water-cooled engine destined for the luxurious Typ 928 coupe.

As early as 1971 there was concern in the U.S. about the handling characteristics of rear-engined cars. In meetings at Weissach, engineers recognized that if the U.S. began legislating automobiles, it would not outlaw water-cooled, front-engined, rear-wheel drive cars produced in Detroit. So in between other projects, Porsche engineers began to conceive and develop the Typ 928.

Design chief Tony Lapine felt obligated to retain the organic, roundness begun with Erwin Komenda's Gmünd coupes. He chal-

1981 B.F.Goodrich 924 Carrera GTR
The Audi-derived Typ 924GTR engine displaced
1,984cc with bore and stroke of 86.5x84.4mm,
producing 375hp at 6400rpm. The single large
KKK turbocharger and intercooler helped to fill the
engine compartment. To eliminate head overheating
problems, a modified water system began the flow
of cooled water directly at the rear of the block.

Handling had been tamed. A new level of luxury had been reached. A front-mounted 4.5-liter 90-degree V-8 offered European markets 240hp, while for the U.S., 225hp came out cleanly through catalytic converters.

Engineers worked to improve performance; engine size jumped to 4.7-liters and then to 5.0-liters in the 1985 928 S models. Dual-overhead cams and four-valves per cylinder increased power again in the 928S4 models for 1987. Production topped 5,400 cars. The S4 performed well: 5.7sec to 60mph and a top speed of 165mph was possible. By 1990, engine output had risen to 326hp for manual transmission versions of the 928GT, providing a top speed of 171mph.

1981 B.F.Goodrich 924 Carrera GTR
A simple, unadorned, single-purpose-built machine,
the 924 GTR was also, at 180,000DM, the most
expensive 924 ever sold. Paul Miller, Pat Bedard, and
Manfred Schurti shared the cockpit until their race
ended when a left-front wheel came off in the early
morning.

lenged the engineers to make the car body act as its own bumper. Fitting in a water-cooling system radiator required other considerations in car bodies previous unperforated. In 1975, engineer Helmut Flegl took over as project manager to continue chassis and drivetrain development. The 928, introduced in Geneva in March 1977, won rave reviews. Appearance was stunning. Performance was impressive.

1981 B.F.Goodrich 924 Carrera GTR

The GTRs hit 180mph along Mulsanne racing on shaved street radial tires. The speed and power were held in check by brakes adapted from the 917 at front and 935 race cars for the rear. The cars weighed 2,196lb without fuel or driver. The bodywork hinted at the production Typ 944 already in development.

1984 Porsche 928S

The 928 was introduced in the fall of 1977, powered by a water-cooled 240hp 4.5-liter V-8. In 1980, the 928S came along with 4.7-liters and a small rear wing to clean up the aerodynamics. By 1980, with the 5.0-liter four-valve engine, performance at last matched the looks.

"Who has the right to define a Porsche only as a rear-engine, air-cooled car? Just because the first two cars were this, can we not grow? Do we not evolve?"

—Ernst Fuhrmann on the 928, from Porsche Legends

Chapter Five

RACING: TRIALS AND TRIUMPHS

Jo Hoppen, Porsche+Audi division competition director for Volkswagen of America had been one of the former guiding lights behind the 1971 and '72 Can-Am successes. In 1978 he visited Ernst Fuhrmann on behalf of American privateer Ted Field who wanted to take Porsche to Indianapolis. It struck Hoppen and Fuhrmann as a good promotional opportunity. The water-cooled-head engine from the Typ 935/78 *Moby Dick*, later used in the Typ 936/78 spyder, was the right size for Indy rules. Field had a Parnelli chassis proven and ready to go. It would require some work but they all reasoned that it could be accomplished by May 1980.

But no one imagined that the United States Auto Club (USAC) was about to be overtaken by Championship Auto Racing Teams (CART), an organization made up of racing team owners, not track owners and promoters. To other competitors, Porsche always represented a serious challenge. Rac-

1990 Porsche March 90P, opposite page
Porsche's Indy engine had an 88.2x54.2mm bore and stroke and produced 725hp at 12,000rpm. It was a dual overhead cam, four-valve-per-cylinder design with a single turbocharger and dual waste gates. Boost was limited to 45in of mercury (3.2 bar) through the pop-off valve atop the intake manifold.

ing history proves that rules could be changed to favor those already inside. So with barely a month to go before the 1980 Indy 500, the turbocharger boost allowance was changed, limiting Porsche to an uncompetitive level. Porsche had not sought an advantage over the other teams, but it had expected an equal opportunity. When that was denied, Porsche withdrew. The four Indy cars went straight into a warehouse.

Changes loomed on the horizon for both production cars and for racing. Similar factors influenced both. A new fuel crunch led to economic uncertainty and inflation. In 1978, the European Carrera was introduced in the U.S. as the 911SC; it was powered by a 3.0-liter 180hp engine. In 1980, 400 copies of a special Weissach commemorative coupe, filled with special trim and details, were produced.

In late 1981 at the Frankfurt auto show, a 930 cabriolet was shown. It would be another two years before the convertible—at first only available in white or red—would be sold. It was Porsche's first true cabrio since the last 356SCs in 1965. The open car was immensely popular. Despite an inflated economy, more than 21,800 cars were sold. Half went to the U.S. and half of those went to Califor-

1980 Interscope Indianapolis
Skilled IMSA-competitor Ted Field sponsored Porsche's first effort to conquer the Indianapolis 500. This attempt used a Parnelli chassis and an engine produced at *Weissach. The 1,496lb car was 36.5in tall, 179in. overall, and rolled on a 104.5in wheelbase.*

nia. The SC designation was dropped in 1984, replaced with the Carrera name as engine displacement increased to 3.2 liters and output rose to 200hp for the U.S. market, 240hp for Europe.

The same environmental and economic concerns that weakened U.S. engines affected FIA rules for racing when Group 5 and 6 were replaced in 1982 with Group C ("consumption"). This was racing meant to be fuel-efficient and environmentally responsible. Limits were placed on how much gasoline could be used in races of set lengths: 600 liters for 1,000km races, 2,800 liters for the 24-hours of LeMans. Engineers at Weissach met the challenge, introducing the Typ 956 in April and winning LeMans with it in June.

FIA specifications for driver safety and cockpit crushability led to an all-new chassis. Norbert Singer's solution was Porsche's first monocoque structure using steel, aluminum, and carbon fiber, surrounded by a Kevlar body. Singer also adopted Formula One technology: the 956 was Porsche's first ground-effects car. The 1,892lb cars used a twin-turbocharged/intercooled version of the 2.65-liter Typ 935/76 engine from the Indy project. It was detuned to 620hp at 8200rpm for endurance races. The cars won in 1983 and 1984 before regulations changed again.

Porsche returned to Formula One racing in 1983, providing its 1.5-liter, 80-degree V-6

1980 Interscope Indianapolis
The Typ 935/78 engine was fitted with water-cooled four-valve cylinder heads. Running a single turbocharger boosted to 54in of mercury (3.85 bar), the 2.65-liter V-8 produced 630hp at 9000rpm on methanol fuel. The heads were welded to the block. Caught by rule changes, it never turned a wheel in anger.

1982 Typ 956
Invented in March 1981 to campaign in the FISA's Group C category, the 956 was an immediate success, winning at LeMans 15 months later. It adopted parts of the ill-fated four-valve Indianapolis engine and the 2.65 liter used in the 1981 version of the 936. The 956 and subsequent Typ 962 went on to win at LeMans six times.

1990 Porsche March 90P, opposite page
Porsche attempted to compete in the CART series again in 1990 but met with frustration. Its 2.65-liter 90-degree V-8 never seemed perfectly mated to March's 90P aluminum-clad, composite materials sandwich monocoque chassis.

1990 Porsche March 90P
The Porsche-March was 183.5in overall on a 112in wheelbase. It was 78.5in wide, 36in tall, and weighed 1,550lb without fuel and driver (Teo Fabi or John Andretti). Two cars attempted the 1990 Indy 500, but neither finished.

TAG TTE-P01 engine for the Techniques Avant Garde McLaren team. The Formula One engine produced 630hp with twin-turbos at 2.5 bar boost. At the hands of drivers Niki Lauda and John Watson, the Porsche engines in McLaren's MP4/1E chassis struggled, but progress through the season was encouraging. For McLaren's 1984 MP4/2 chassis, boost on the TAG-P01 was raised to 3.2 bar and power increased to 750bhp. Changes and improvements yielded spectacular results: McLaren (with Alain Prost replacing Watson) won the constructors championship and Lauda won The World Driving Championship with Prost finishing second behind him. Between the beginning of 1984 and the end of '87, Porsche and McLaren scored twenty-five GP victories. With those results Porsche once again yielded to the temptation of Indianapolis.

At the end of the 1987 CART season, the Typ 2708 2.65-liter 90-degree V-8 engine was mated to Porsche's own full carbon-fiber monocoque chassis. The engine produced 750hp at 11,200rpm at 48in (3.4 bar) of boost. Plagued by chassis stiffness problems, Porsche bought a March 88C chassis for the next year. Chassis problems continued until 1989's March 89P chassis put team driver Teo Fabi on the pole at Portland and left him first overall at Mid-Ohio. But reproducing the four-year run of success that Porsche had achieved internationally in Formula One proved elusive once again in U.S. Indy Car racing. The March 90P chassis and Typ 2708 engine, limited to 45in (3.2 bar) of boost, (producing 725hp at 12,000rpm) never quite worked perfectly. Porsche threw up its hands in frustration and withdrew from the series before the end of the 1990 season.

New IMSA rules dictated that a driver's feet must be behind the front wheel axle beginning with the 1987 season. This was adopted by the international governing bodies. The 956 wheelbase could not be lengthened because of the monocoque. As 956s crashed or teams ordered new cars, new Typ 962s were delivered as replacements. The factory raced its 962s at LeMans in 1987 and finished first, second, and third. And then Porsche withdrew, leaving endurance racing to its customers.

1990 Porsche March 90P

Teo Fabi pulled out of the pits during open practice before the first qualifying weekend. He qualified in 2min, 43.62sec, at 220.022mph. The cars were fitted with five-speed transmissions which failed on Fabi's car after 162 laps.

Chapter Six

STRETCHING THE ROAD CARS

In 1986, Porsche reintroduced the 911 Turbo to the U.S. market as a coupe, Targa, and a cabriolet, fulfilling the prophesy shown at the Frankfurt show in 1983. The Typ 959, a technology showcase also introduced at Frankfurt, was offered for public sale in 1987, albeit to a small, well-heeled crowd.

The 959 grew from the same inspiration that led Ferdinand Piëch to imagine the 911R and Ernst Fuhrmann to create the 2.7 RS and 930 Turbo. How far was it possible to take the 911? How fast? How advanced?

Peter Schutz, Porsche's then president, an American and a car lover, agreed with engineering chief Helmuth Bott that the 911 should go on and must go far. A prototype model, Typ 953, raced and won the 1984 Paris-Dakar rally. A Typ 961 road race version competed in Germany. When the four-wheel

1993 America GS Hardtop Roadster, opposite page
Porsche Customer Service, for customers of sufficient means, will delete undercoatings, adapt body panels from various models, install electronics suitable to monitor space flight, (and create power enough to assist it) and it will encourage the inventors, thinkers, and tinkerers from Zuffenhausen and Weissach to stretch their imaginations and to leap far beyond the normal production limitations.

drive six-speed Kevlar-bodied 959 appeared for sale in 1987, it accelerated to 60mph in 3.7sec and had a top speed of nearly 200mph. This was a production car meant for public roads. Only 224 were produced (including twenty-four prototypes to make certain that the ultimate 911 delivered on every promise). Porsche's unwillingness to bend to U.S. regulatory intransigence kept the car from American buyers except in the case of public museums and collections. Although fully legal elsewhere, for years these cars could be driven in the U.S. only with special permits on demonstration runs.

Just as the 959s were first sold in 1987, the 911 Speedster, another Bott/Schutz collaboration, was introduced at Frankfurt. Two prototype versions were blended into the final production model from which a limited run of 2,100 cars were finally sold.

The Typ 924 was replaced by the 944 in 1983, offered as a coupe and cabriolet; eventually a turbocharged version was also built. The 944 was replaced by the Typ 968 in 1991, fitted with a version of the six-speed transmission from the 959. At the same time, Porsche introduced the Typ 964 Carrera 2 and Carrera 4 models. These used a 3.6-liter

1988 Typ 959 U.S. Sport, above

The appearance of the 959 is testimony to styling chief Tony Lapine's ability to fulfill company president Peter Schutz and engineer Helmuth Bott's request for an ultimate 911 that would not betray the familiar lines. The body is steel, fiberglass, and Kevlar; the suspension is active and interacts with full-time active four-wheel-drive and anti-lock brakes. The car sold new for 430,000DM.

1988 Typ 959 U.S. Sport, left

The Typ 959/50 engine is 2.85 liters with 95x67mm bore and stroke. With electronic ignition and twin water-cooled turbochargers, 450hp is achieved at 6500rpm. Plumbing for the turbochargers is complex and fills much of the compartment.

normally aspirated air-cooled engine producing 247hp. Coupes, cabriolets and Targas could reach 60mph in 5.5sec and topped at 162mph. A Tiptronic transmission reinvented the Sportomatic semi-automatic gear box from the 1970s, but it was only available for the Carrera 2.

1989 Porsche 911 Speedster
Envisioned by Helmuth Bott, Tony Lapine, and Peter Schutz, the 911 Speedster adopted styling cues from other models and introduced the "camel humps" tonneau behind the seats. Around 2,100 were produced using the 3.2-liter flat-six mated to a five-speed transmission. Top speed was nearly 150mph.

1990 Porsche 930 Turbo Cabrio Flatnose
Working with engineer Rolf Sprenger's Sonderwunsch—special wishes—program in customer service, anything is possible if the client is willing and able. When the last regular production Typ 930 Turbo Cabriolet was purchased, the owner was intrigued by possibilities. Options opened up that had never before existed.

Special Wishes

The Customer Service department at Zuffenhausen has a program called *Sonderwunsch* (Special Wishes) that for decades has customized paint and interior trim to match clothing or even hair or eye color. It performs engine modifications and has detuned and modified racing cars like the 917K and 935 to street use. The final production turbo cabriolet, purchased by an American customer, set engineer Rolf Sprenger's Customer Service department reaching farther than ever before. The car was

fitted with acres of black leather and hundreds of never-before dreamed-of ideas and conveniences. A moisture sensor automatically raises the top and windows, arms the alarm, and notifies the owner of rain by remote pager.

Sprenger and his workers vowed never again to undertake anything so complex. But another opportunity arose. Inspired by Chief Stylist Harm Lagaay's Porsche PanAmericana built for Ferry Porsche's 80th birthday present, the owner of the final flatnose approached

1993 America GS Hardtop Roadster
Beginning with a Carrera 2 wide body cabriolet, the America GS roadster evolved. Incredibly, its removable steel hardtop has a fully retracting electric sunroof and an electrically heated rear window. Electric contacts in the roof pillars and the roadster body provide the electricity.

1993 America GS Hardtop Roadster, above
The all-leather center console houses a graphic equalizer and numerous other spoiler, telephone, and security controls. Leather was specially dyed green and purple to specification, all supervised by Porsche chief stylist Harm Lagaay and executed by Rolf Sprenger's customer service staff.

Sprenger and *Sonderwunsch* again. Lagaay got involved. The result, after nearly four years work, was a kind of prototype for the 40th Anniversary issue of 250 America Roadsters. These were based on Carrera 2 wide-body cabriolets. The America GS (Grand Sport) Hardtop Roadster, challenged Sprenger's engineers. The idea was to recreate and update the 1950s sports cars that were driven to the track and raced all day. The GS's mechanical running gear is either Carrera 3.8-liter RS or RSR. It uses a racing Sportomatic gearbox, has no insulation or undercoating, no power steering or air conditioning, and has external electric kill switches. Carrera RSR Recaro racing bucket seats are leather covered. Its engineering piece-de-resistance is its removable hardtop that incorporates an electric sliding sun roof and electrically heated rear window.

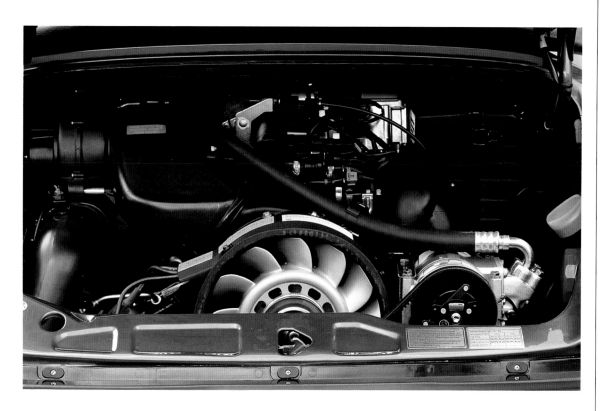

1993 America GS Hardtop Roadster, previous page
The GS is fitted with a Carrera 3.8 RS engine and a racing version of the Tiptronic transmission to get nearly 300hp to the ground. Chassis and suspension modifications parallel those in the RS as well. Custom BBS 18in wheels hold Pirelli P-Zero tires all around.

1993 America GS Hardtop Roadster, above
The car's design was inspired by Ferry Porsche's eightieth birthday present, the PanAmericana showcar. It became a prototype for the 40th Anniversary America Roadsters. Production of this car took forty-four months.

1990 Porsche 930 Turbo Cabrio Flatnose
From its flachtbau—*flat nose—to its tea-tray tail, nearly everything imaginable was touched on the car. The build sheet specifying the options fitted to the car* *ran to more than eleven pages. Leather abounds. Stereo sound quality is better than some recording studios. The car took two years to complete.*

1990 Porsche 930 Turbo Cabrio Flatnose, left
Engine modifications are possible, although for the U.S. market cars they are few and minor. Engine out-put, aided by Bosch's Motronic Engine Management System, is reportedly more than 450hp at 6500rpm. A six-speed transmission from the Typ 959 was fitted to a Quaiffe differential to take better advantage of the engine's improved performance.

1990 Porsche 930 Turbo Cabrio Flatnose
The already hand-built 930 cabriolet was virtually completely reassembled after chassis modification and suspension improvements were complete. Special instrumentation was added, some adapted from race cars, others from air craft. A moisture sensor will raise the top and windows, arm the alarm, and notify the owner by remote pager of the change in weather.

1993 Porsche 3.8-liter RSR, left
The new FIA-Super Car contender 3.8-liter RSR sits in front of a 1969 911R, the car that inspired many of the "silhouette" racers that have evolved within bodies from production cars. Doors and front deck lid are aluminum. The European Super Car Championship versions are U.S. race-eligible.

Porsche announced in 1989 that the 911 Turbo would be discontinued. A new version on a new chassis would be introduced in the future, but the new car could accommodate neither the cabriolet body style nor the Typ 935 flatnose modification due to redesigned suspension geometry and engine oil cooling.

Just two years later, in 1991, the Turbo was reintroduced for 1992, using a 3.3-liter intercooled engine producing 315hp. At Frankfurt Porsche also introduced its Boxster, a mid-engine design study meant for possible production as an affordable Porsche (around

1993 Porsche 3.8-liter RSR
Derived from production cars, the center console parcel tray is retained as is a quite-standard-looking instrument panel. On-board fire-extinguisher lines surround the driver's Recaro competition racing shell. The car is limited by rules to a minimum weight of 2,464lb. Options include an air jack system.

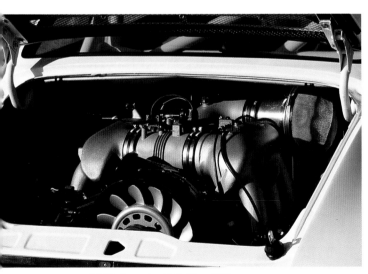

1993 Porsche 3.8-liter RSR
Normal breathing seldom looks like this. The enormous air-intake covered with fine mesh allows engine sound to flood the cockpit. The mechanical crash and clatter of internal combustion at idle is such that inexperienced drivers wonder if the engine is self-destructing.

$40,000 U.S.). Porsche intends to counter the effective engineering and marketing competition from Japanese car makers. The Boxster, styled as a strict two-seater, is reminiscent of the Typ RS-60 spyder. Porsche also introduced the Carrera 3.8-liter RS and the RSR, meant for competition in the popular European Super Car Championships. The 2,462lb RSRs use a 3.75-liter 325hp Typ M64/04 flat-six with dual ignition. RSRs placed first in GT class at LeMans in 1993 and first, second, and third (eighth, ninth, and tenth overall) in 1994. The 300hp road version of the RS sells for 220,000DM in Germany and weighs only 172lb more than the RSR. But it is not yet legal in the U.S.

Beginning in 1992, Dauer, a specialty shop in Germany, began to modify 962 race cars for European road use. Enough of these were sold that it qualified for GT class racing (Norbert Singer discovered that beneficial loophole). Porsche entered two Weissach-prepared Dauer 962LMs in the GT class. And following a long factory absence at LeMans, Porsche placed first and third overall in 1994. It was the firm's first victory there in seven years.

Over the past twenty-five years Porsche has suffered fits and starts. Hammered by the economy and challenged by aggressive competition, it has survived circumstances that have damaged other companies badly. Its problems are not over, but Porsche is still made up of passionate engineers deeply in love with the automobile. This great resource keeps Porsche at the top of the list of cars coveted by enthusiasts, admired by journalists, and respected by racers.

1993 Porsche 3.8-liter RSR

The two-deck plastic wing is a signature-piece of the racing RSR and its detuned road version RS. Unhappily for U.S. drivers, the RS is not legal. The 3,746cc RSR engine, Typ M64/06, produces 325hp at 6900rpm. The 5-speed transmission is connected to a 40-percent limited slip and, depending on the gearing, offers a top speed of at least 165mph.

INDEX